Augustus C. Merriam

The Greek and Latin Inscriptions on the Obelisk-Crab

in the Metropolitan Museum, New York. A monograph.

Augustus C. Merriam

The Greek and Latin Inscriptions on the Obelisk-Crab
in the Metropolitan Museum, New York. A monograph.

ISBN/EAN: 9783337418649

Printed in Europe, USA, Canada, Australia, Japan

Cover: Foto ©ninafisch / pixelio.de

More available books at **www.hansebooks.com**

THE GREEK AND LATIN INSCRIPTIONS

ON THE

OBELISK - CRAB

IN THE

METROPOLITAN MUSEUM, NEW YORK

A Monograph

By AUGUSTUS C. MERRIAM, Ph.D.

ADJUNCT PROFESSOR OF GREEK IN COLUMBIA COLLEGE

NEW YORK

HARPER & BROTHERS, FRANKLIN SQUARE

1883

PREFACE.

Of the two obelisks at Alexandria, Egypt, which for so long divided
the interest of tourists with Pompey's Pillar, one lay prostrate upon
the ground, the other, though erect, was hidden for some feet above
its base-stone by the accumulation of *débris* about it. When Mr.
Dixon was preparing, in 1877, to remove the fallen monolith to England, he excavated about the base of the other in order to ascertain
what kind of a pedestal had originally supported the obelisk. In
doing so he discovered that it had rested upon four bronze sea-crabs,
two of which alone remained in place, the other pair having been
wrenched out and carried off, apparently by plunderers. One of
those still in position had lost both claws and all the legs, only the
stumps of these remaining. The other had been mutilated very
similarly, but the right claw in part was still left, and upon this had
been engraved a Greek and a Latin inscription. These crabs were
removed by Commander Gorringe with the obelisk to this city in
1880, and were presented by him to the Metropolitan Museum of
Art in Central Park in June, 1881. The Annual Report of the
Museum, made public on the 12th of February, 1883, contained the
following paragraph: "In the last Report we acknowledged the gift
of two bronze crabs, found at Alexandria, as supports to the obelisk
now in Central Park, on one of which were inscriptions. Restrictions
imposed by the donor against copying or publishing the inscriptions
for a certain time having been recently removed, they have been
copied, and impressions, photographs, and sketches made for the
study of scholars. These fail to confirm the accuracy of the readings which have been published."

One of the sketches here mentioned was sent to Dr. F. A. P. Barnard, President of Columbia College, and led to an investigation, the results of which are contained in this publication. The form which the last originally assumed, of a record of advance in discovery, has been retained for many reasons. All investigation must be made with some groping, not with full knowledge. The introduction thus given behind the scenes, as it were, may dispel some of the illusion of stage scenery, but may also win credit where doubt will be eager to fasten.

My thanks are due to President Barnard, for his interest in the matter, to Professor H. Drisler, for many suggestions as to the consultation of authorities, to Professors J. W. White of Harvard and M. Warren of Johns Hopkins, for the loan of books, and to R. S. Poole and W. Henzen, for information duly acknowledged below.

Augustus C. Merriam.

Department of Greek, Columbia College,
N. Y., *June* 5, 1883.

COLUMBIA COLLEGE,
DEPARTMENT OF GREEK,
May 9th, 1883.

President F. A. P. BARNARD:

Dear Sir,—Your attention having been called some time in January last to certain discrepancies existing between the inscriptions on the bronze crab found under our obelisk at Alexandria and the versions published here,' Professor Drisler requested me to investigate the matter, which I accordingly did, and now have the honor to submit the following report.

As a preliminary, it became necessary to consult Commander Gorringe's "Egyptian Obelisks," where I found the inscriptions given in this form:

L. Η ΚΑΙΣΑΡΟΣ	ANNO VIII
ΒΑΡΒΑΡΟΣ ΑΝΕΘΗΚΕ	AVGVSTI CAESARIS
ΑΡΧΙΤΕΚΤΟΝ ΟΥΝΤΟΣ	BARBARVS PRAEF
ΠΟΝΤΙΟΥ	AEGYPTI POSVIT
	ARCHITECTANTE PONTIO

On the 27th of January I visited the Museum, and spent some time in making a transcript from the bronze of all that could be easily deciphered. The condition then presented by the inscriptions as far as I observed will be seen in the accompanying fac-similes (a) (a), with the three exceptions which will be noted below.

The portion of the claw of the crab now remaining, upon which the inscriptions are engraved, is eight and three quarters inches in

---

' So far as I know, these inscriptions were first published here by G. L. Feuardent, from a paper read before the American Numismatic and Archaeological Society of New York, on the 15th of January, 1881, and printed during the same year. This paper is embodied in the main in Commander Gorringe's "Obelisks," the form of the inscriptions being the same in both. At the commencement of this investigation I was not aware that they had ever been published abroad. Vague rumors to the effect that they had appeared in some foreign journal I was unable to verify until my own inquiries were completed. See pp. 34.

length, and seven and three quarters in width. The Greek on the outside occupies a space of about eight inches in length by three and one half in width; the Latin, within, five and three quarters by three inches; both being cut upon a convex surface. The Greek, as a whole, is in a fine state of preservation. The letters are deeply and accurately cut, in the main, and their exact size may be seen on the fac-simile. Between the L and H rises a knob of the crab about an inch in diameter at the base, and a similar one stands between the H and K following. The Σ at the end of the first line was smaller than the other letters, and represented by irregular lines, slightly but plainly cut. Σ of ΒΑΡΒΑΡΟΣ was clearly outlined, but filled entirely to the surface with oxidation.[1] E at the end of the second line is engraved partly on the curve where the bronze begins to round at the extremity between the two nippers, which were about one and one half inch apart here. In the next line the final Σ is cut entirely on the end, and but roughly at that; hence it does not appear in a squeeze at all.

The Latin is inscribed on the inside of the claw, opposite to the Greek, but between the shoulder and the curved and projecting nippers, which are now gone. In studying the form of the letters it is necessary to take this into consideration; and also the fact that the other claw, now gone, stretched out within twenty inches of it at the base or shoulder, and, to judge from the restorations now under the obelisk, within about thirteen inches at the extremity of the nippers. This confined position gave the workman less freedom in the employment of his tools, and the letters are smaller, less deeply cut, irregular in shape, and poorly executed; while the lines do not run straight across like those of the Greek, but slant considerably upward from left to right. The surface of the bronze on this side has suffered severe injuries from deep cuts and scratches, as well as from pounding or other violence. Some of these cuts, though not wide enough themselves to destroy the letters completely, have actually produced this effect by the fact that the upturned furrows have been driven down over the adjacent surface. AESARIS is plainly cut, and the C before it clearly outlined by a color mark, but the surface

---

[1] For convenience of space this is drawn in the fac-simile, as it now appears.

(a)

ΗΟΚΛΛΙΛΜΡΣ
ΒΑΡΒΑΡΟΣ ΑΝΕΘΗΚΕ
ΑΡΧΙΤΕΚΤΟΝΟΥΝΤΟΣ
ΠΟΝΤΙΟΥ

ΗΟΚΛΛΙΣΜΡΣ

(b)

CAESARIS

(a)

...SA... A...FVS PRAEF
AEGYPTI DPOSVIT A
ARCHITECTANE PONTIO

...III CAESARIS
...BA FVS PRAEF

(BARBA...)

(b)

to the left of this is badly marred. In the next line was a curious combination of letters and marks, some of the latter impossible to catch at all except in certain lights. Towards the end, RAEF was plain enough, and before it the top of a P distinctly engraved, though the remainder is completely destroyed by a deep triangular gouge. Enough remains of the P to render it a certain letter. The A at the beginning of the last line was difficult to make out, so that I did not draw it; but it is now added in the fac-simile.

It was easy to see at a glance that the inscriptions presented considerable difficulties, and the discrepancies between them and the published readings were such as to render necessary a complete reconsideration of the subject, historically and epigraphically.

We will begin, then, with the Greek, since the reading there is more certain, in consequence of the surface having suffered less injury.

At the first blush, a character with the form of a Latin L in a Greek inscription with no archaic characteristics, strikes one as something anomalous; and so it would be in general in an inscription from Greece proper; but we are well aware that this is from Egypt, where the L is known to occur frequently. Our great storehouse of Greek inscriptions is Boeckh's "Corpus Inscriptionum Graecarum" (cited below as the "Corpus" or as "C. I."), in four volumes folio, the third volume of which was published in 1853 under the editorship of J. Franz. This contains such inscriptions as had been discovered in Egypt up to that time, gathered from the works of various travellers, but based mainly upon Letronne's "Recueil des Inscrip. Grecq. et Lat. de l'Égypte" (1842-8). The collection of Franz amounts to some three hundred in number, to which may be added about one hundred and fifty more from the adjacent region of Ethiopia. A very large part of these are dated in the year of the Ptolemaic king or Roman emperor during whose reign the inscription was made, and the great majority of such have the word for year indicated by this character L. The date itself commonly follows the L, expressed in the usual Greek manner by the letters of the Greek alphabet. Rarely the letters precede the L. That this character represents the word for year there is now no possibility of doubt, but its precise origin, and the exact word in Greek for which it stands, are points about which there has been considerable dispute ever since the revival of learning. It seems to have attracted attention first upon coins, where it occurs frequently among those struck by the Ptolemies and the Roman emperors, and it was conjectured to be the initial of the Greek ΛΥΚΑΒΑΣ, an archaic and poetic word for year. Such is the explanation of H. Goltz in his work on coins published in 1574. J. J. Scaliger, however, in 1583 and again in 1609 tried to prove that it represented the Latin *Lustrum*, a space of five years, meeting the objection that this would make the reigns of the emperors too long, by asserting that the coins on which such dates were found did not give the year of the emperor, but that of the imposition of tribute upon the particular city in question, and he indulges in some ridicule of those *learned* men who persist in opposing his theory. But this supposition could not maintain itself long, as the collections of coins increased so that wider and more accurate surveys of the field could be made. And yet, Casaubon is said by Placentius to have acceded to it at one time; at another, according to Noris, he thought it a mark used to separate words or letters from one another. But this was refuted by the fact that it often occurs where no word or letter precedes. In spite of various other opinions ΛΥΚΑΒΑΣ held its ground, Hardouin in 1685 stating that the L was the Latin letter, but in 1689 recalling this opinion, on the ground that it was found on the coins of the Ptolemies anterior to any Roman influence through which the Latin L could have been borrowed, and explaining, that L was not only a Latin but also an archaic Greek character (as is well known now, of course), and that it had been purposely chosen instead of the common Λ as the initial representative of ΛΥΚΑΒΑΣ in order to avoid confusion. Was the year 32, for instance, to be written, it might be expressed by LΛB, instead of ΛΛB. Vaillant, in 1692, explains simply as ΛΥΚΑΒΑΣ, but Noris in 1729 suggests that it stands rather for ΕΤΟΣ, the ordinary Greek word for year. His main argument for this is drawn from an old manuscript in the library of the Grand Duke of Tuscany, formerly belonging to Angelus Politianus, and containing various tracts on astronomy. The next page to the last of this manuscript contained some signs under a Greek title meaning, " Explanation of Signs Used;" and among the signs this: LL, ΕΤΗ. Hence, as several of the

signs there found are not Latin, and as astronomy was especially an
Egyptian science, he concludes that the Egyptians designated the
year by the mark L, and from there its use extended into Syria: and
that this character is a mere conventional sign, and not a letter at all.
But still, ΛΥΚΑΒΑΣ maintained its supremacy, as with Placentius,
1757, and Rasche, 1785; while Eckhel in 1797 regards it as tri-
umphantly proved by "the recent discovery" of ΛΥΚΑΒΑΝΤΟΣ
ΔΕΚΑΤΟΥ on an Alexandrian coin of Vespasian. He is followed by
Champollion in 1819, and Letronne in his "Recueil," 1848, vol. ii.
p. 129; but on page 450 he deserts ΛΥΚΑΒΑΣ altogether; for he has
now met with two inscriptions[1] which read, TO ΙΔ L KAI ΙΕ L, and
ΑΠΟ ΤΟΥ ϛ L ΕΙΣ ΤΟ ΙΗ, respectively, where the *neuter* article shows
that the *neuter* word ΕΤΟΣ, and not the *masculine* ΛΥΚΑΒΑΣ, was
present to the mind of the writer. From this he arrives at the same
conclusion as Noris, that L is a conventional sign for ΕΤΟΣ, as ⊢ for
the drachma, and C for the obol. The period of neither of these inscriptions can be fixed with certainty, which may be said also of C. I.
No. 4862b, which exhibits a similar use of the article. But Peyron,
in his "Papiri Greci del Mus. Brit." (1841), gives the transcripts of
several Greek papyri of about 164 B.C., in the reign of Ptolemy Philo-
metor. In the third of these, the article occurs once in the same form
of expression as above, in the sixth six times,[2] in the ninth once, in
the tenth twice. The second papyrus is given, in part, C. I. iii. p. 301.
It consists of a petition addressed to the king by Ptolemy, the son of
Glaucias, a Macedonian, who begs, as a reward for having lived as a
religious recluse for fifteen years at the temple of Serapis in Memphis,[3]
that his younger brother may receive an appointment as officer in the
army. He writes the "fifteen years" in the form ετη ιε. His brother
gives the petition to the king, who countersigns it and refers the
matter to the scribes in the proper department. There an official
digest of the petition is made by the scribes, in which the ετη ιε of
Ptolemy is written L ιε.[4] All this tends to prove that at that
early period ΕΤΟΣ and not ΛΥΚΑΒΑΣ was understood to be repre-

---

[1] C. I. No. 4684d, and 4716d³⁹.

[2] το ηι L, εις το ιθ L. No accents or breathings are found in these papyri.

[3] συμβαντος δε γεγονεναι με εν κατοχηι εν τωι προς μεμφει μεγαλωι σαραπιειωι ετη ιε.

[4] εγραφει ειναι εν κατοχη εν τω προς μεμφει μεγαλωι σαραπιειωι L ιε.

12

sented by L. Franz had already reached this conclusion in 1840[1] and afterwards regarded the arguments of Letronne as convincing proof;[2] and Gardthausen[3] gives "L, ΕΤΟΥΣ, ΕΤΗ," among a number of "conventional hieroglyphic" signs, and refers to Letronne's earlier interpretation (ΛΥΚΑΒΑΣ) as a false one. Furthermore, against the single coin of Vespasian containing ΛΥΚΑΒΑΝΤΟΣ, great numbers can be cited of various ages with ΕΤΟΣ or some abbreviation of this word; and of all the seventeen inscriptions given by Boeckh in which ΛΥΚΑΒΑΣ is employed for "year," though gathered from diverse parts of the Greek world, every single one is poetic.

If we may rely at this day upon the labors of Rasche, Eckhel, Mionnet, etc., we may conclude that this L appears first on the coins of Ptolemy I., and to him the honor would be due of having introduced into numismatics so convenient a character, after he had bestowed upon Egypt the great boon of a uniform system of coinage, and, becoming actual king of the country, he began to date his years from the death of Alexander. From Egypt its use would be extended to Cyprus, Syria, Cyrene, and all that region of the Levant over which the Ptolemies held sway. From coins it passed into ordinary use in writing and inscriptions, but was mainly confined throughout its history to Egypt and its adjacent regions.[4]

So far then, L H of our inscription reads according to the full Greek expression, ΕΤΟΥΣ ΟΓΔΟΟΥ, "in the eighth year;" for in these

---

[1] Element. Epigr. Graec. p. 375.

[2] C. I. iii. p. 1186.

[3] Griechische Palaeog. 1879.

[4] In answer to a letter of inquiry respecting the earliest appearance of this character on coins, Mr. Reginald Stuart Poole, of the British Museum, has since written me as follows: "The earliest occurrence I know of in coins of the symbol L is on those of Ptolemy Philopator, dated in his third year, and issued in Cyprus (Catalogue Ptol., Intr., p. l., Tables, p. 62). The date is B.C 220–219. The symbol, I think, is derived from the demotic form of the Egyptian (hieroglyphic) symbol for the year ⸢, which is ⸢ L in hieratic, and ⸣ ⸣ in demotic. I admit that the demotic form seems too remote for the L, but the demotic could always typically recall its hieratic prototype." Mr. Poole has just been engaged in issuing the Catalogue of Ptolemaic Coins to which he alludes, and his identifications are based on a more exact and comprehensive study than that of his predecessors, while his acquaintance with Egyptology renders his derivation of the symbol especially interesting and valuable.

dates the Greek letters represent the ordinal and not the cardinal numbers, a fact sometimes more clearly indicated, as in the coin of Vespasian cited above, as well as in other ways.

Next we pass on to ΚΑΙΣΑΡ Σ. That this is meant for ΚΑΙΣΑΡΟΣ, "of Cæsar," is beyond question, both from the analogy of other inscriptions, and from the position of the final Σ, which leaves room for a small o, which was very commonly employed in such expressions, and might possibly be revealed here by removal of the incrustation on the surface. There certainly was not room for both Ο and Σ to be cut, of the same size as the other letters of the word; and if the Ο was omitted altogether, it is not without numerous precedents, as C. I. 4715 (an inscription in honor of Augustus), where we read without variant ΑΥΤΟΚΡΑΤΟΡΟΣ, but Wescher corrects to ΑΥΤΟΚΡΑΤΟΡΣ, as actually found.

ΚΑΙΣΑΡΟΣ, then, "of Cæsar;" but of what Cæsar in the long line from Julius down? Since neither inscription answers the question directly, the solution must be obtained by a comparison of other inscriptions and the habitual methods there employed in such designations, together with such facts of history as may be brought to bear upon the matter in hand. Julius Cæsar is excluded by the fact that his connection with Egypt extended only from 48 to 44 B.C., a period too short for an eighth year. But ancient authorities tell us that Augustus conquered Egypt B.C. 30, that the line of Ptolemaic rulers became extinct in effect upon the death of Cleopatra shortly after Augustus entered Alexandria, and that the country was reduced to the form of a Roman province under a Roman governor, called *præfectus* during all the earlier period, but *præfectus Augustalis* or simply *Augustalis*, later on. Upon examining the inscriptions from this region in the "Corpus," it is found that all those which, by the length of the reign indicated,' as well as for epigraphic reasons and other circumstances, must be assigned to Augustus, have Cæsar alone, without any further designation of his name: while the other emperors have each his proper name or names in addition to that of Cæsar. This has led Letronne, Franz, and other authorities to assign to

' Nos. 4715, 4909, 4929b, 4929c, in the 31st year, 5086 in the 32d, 4863 in the 35th, 4922 in the 38th, 4716d' in the 43d.

Augustus all inscriptions where Cæsar alone occurs, unless some
very strong reason opposes.   Twice only throughout the Egyptian
section of the "Corpus" has this emperor any distinctive name but
Cæsar, and that on the Nilometer where he is called ΑΥΓΟΥΣΤΟΣ
ΚΑΙΣΑΡ (not ΣΕΒΑΣΤΟΣ).   A good example of the difference in this
respect between him and his successors is to be found ĩn C. I. 4716d¹
and 4716d².   In the former, a person named Agathapous pays his
adoration to Pan in the forty-third year of Cæsar (L ΜΓ ΚΑΙΣΑΡΟΣ);
and in the second, the same individual in the same place three or four
years after offers his vows in the fifth year of *Tiberius* Cæsar (ΕΤΟΥΣ
Ε ΤΙΒΕΡΙΟΥ ΚΑΙΣΑΡΟΣ).   From such evidence it is safe to conclude
that the crab inscription refers to Augustus Cæsar.

Accordingly, the next point to determine is the year from which his
reign began to be reckoned.   There was the Actian Era, dating from
31 B.C., and the Augustan Era, dating from 27 B.C., when Octavianus
received the title of Augustus.   But, in fact, that it is neither of these
which was regularly employed in Egypt becomes plain from the
following evidence:

Alexandria was captured August 1st, B.C. 30, and as soon as the
news reached Rome the Senate, Dio Cassius tells us, decreed that
"the day on which Alexandria was taken should be a holiday,
and the computation of their years should be made from that day."¹
When Censorinus says (De Die Natal. 21) that the Egyptians began
their era two years earlier than the Romans did their Augustan Era,
because Egypt was reduced two years before Octavianus was styled
Augustus, he is not very wide of the mark; in reality, it was two
years and some months, and the decree of the Senate was not carried
into effect in precise terms; for it was arranged that the year
should begin on the 29th of August, the Egyptian New-Year's day,
as Ideler showed conclusively by his exhaustive treatment of the
subject in his "Historische Untersuchungen," 1806, where he verified
the statements of the Ptolemaic Canon by various astronomical cal-
culations.   He conjectures with probability that Cleopatra's death
did not actually occur till about the 29th of August.   Philo Judæus,

¹ li. 19: τήν τε ἡμίραν ἐν ᾗ ἡ Ἀλεξάνϕεια ἑάλω, ἀγαϑήν τε εἶναι καὶ ἐς τὰ ἐπειτα ἐτη ἀρχήν τῆς ἀπαριϑμήσεως αὐτῶν νομίζεσϑαι.

Clemens Alexandrinus, and Ptolemy, all natives of Alexandria, say that Augustus ruled over Egypt forty-three years, which would be exactly the case, within a few hours at least, according to one of their systems in which the New-Year's day was allowed to fall one day earlier every four years, instead of intercalating a day for leap-year. If further proof were necessary, it is furnished by the inscription mentioned above as erected by Agathapous in the forty-third year of Augustus, in the month *Phamenoth*, corresponding to our February or March. Reckoning from August 29th, B.C. 30, the forty-third year is A.D. 14, and Augustus died on the 19th of August, A.D. 14. Agathapous builded better than he knew.

Hence, when an Egyptian date in the reign of Augustus is given without the month, as on the crab, it is impossible to determine to which of two years of our era it belongs, since the first third of the Egyptian year fell into one, and the remainder into the other. Consequently, the "eighth year" must be indicated by 23–22 B.C.

Another point must here be mentioned. In the large majority of instances throughout the inscriptions the date is placed at the end instead of the beginning, as on the crab; but the following may be cited where it stands at the beginning: C. I. 4701, 4737, 4863, 4963, 4980, 4984, 4989, 4994, 4996, 5004, 5010.

The next question for consideration is whether Barbarus was the prefect. Of this the Greek says nothing; the Latin evidently had some name before the word PRAEF, but it seemed to demand considerable boldness, not to say rashness, to make BARBARVS out of the inarticulate combination of letters and marks presented by the bronze, unless some substantial proof could be presented that BARBARVS *ought* to be there. Hence, we must turn to history and see if Barbarus could have been prefect in 23–22. All authorities agree that the first prefect appointed over Egypt by Augustus was Cornelius Gallus, the friend and patron of Virgil; that his term of office lasted till 26 B.C.,[1] when he became intoxicated by the almost unlimited power in his hands, began to set up statues of himself, inscribe his exploits upon the pyramids, and play the king indeed; that he was thereupon recalled by Augustus, and soon put an end to his life

---

[1] Dio Cassius, liii. 23.

by his own hand. In relation to his successor, authorities are no longer at one, some asserting that he was Ælius Gallus, others Petronius. A careless expression of Dio's lies at the root of the trouble; but the question is hardly worth discussing here, since the evidence is overwhelming that Petronius was prefect in 24, when Ælius Gallus led the expedition into Arabia Felix, some of the flutter of which at Rome we see even in the lines of Horace[1] and Virgil.[2] Josephus tells us[3] that a great famine fell upon the Jews in the thirteenth year of Herod, and continued with such severity that in the following season, when it was ascertained that the grain which had been sowed the previous year had perished in the ground, Herod melted down his plate, and sent the proceeds for corn to his friend Petronius, who held the prefecture of Egypt under appointment from Augustus;[4] and again,[5] that the battle of Actium, B.C. 31, occurred in the seventh year of Herod. Hence Petronius was prefect in 24, and the language of Josephus intimates that he was prefect still earlier,[6] as he probably had been ever since the deposition of Cornelius Gallus. This follows also from the language of Strabo,[7] and surely no writer had a better knowledge of that region and time than this geographer. He lived for some time in Alexandria, was a particular friend of Ælius Gallus, and made his tour through Egypt in company with him when Ælius was prefect, as he distinctly states.[8] Augustus returned from Spain to Rome in 24, probably in January;[9] and in the early part of this year, or even earlier,[10] the Capitol was astir with thoughts of the Arabian expedition; and, as Josephus says,[11] it was "about the time" when Petronius sent the corn to Herod, that the latter dispatched five hundred auxiliaries to join this expedition, which was to have sailed, as it would seem, towards the last of July

---

[1] C. i. 29.   [2] Aen. vii. 605.   [3] Antiq. Jud. xv. 9, 1–2.

[4] ἔπεμπε δ᾽ ἐπ᾽ Αἰγύπτου τὰ χρήματα, Πετρωνίου τὴν ἐπαρχίαν ἀπὸ Καίσαρος εἰληφότος.

[5] Antiq. Jud. xv. 5, 2.

[6] xv. 9, 2 : οὗτος οὐκ ὀλίγων ἐπ᾽ αὐτὸν καταφευγόντων διὰ τὰς αὐτὰς χρείας, ἰδίᾳ τε φίλος ὢν Ἡρώδῃ, καὶ διασώσασθαι θέλων τοὺς ὑπ᾽ αὐτῷ, π ρ ώ τ ο ι ς μὲν ἔδωκεν ἐξάγειν τὸν σῖτον, εἰς ἅπαντα δὲ κατὰ τὴν ὠνὴν καὶ τὸν ἐκπλουν συνήργησεν, ὡς μέγα μέρος ἢ τὸ πᾶν γενέσθαι ταύτης τῆς βοηθείας.

[7] Strabo, 118, 819, and throughout his Geography.   [8] Strabo, 118.

[9] Dio, liii. 28.   [10] Hor. i. 35 ; Dio, liii. 22.

[11] xv. 9, 3 : περὶ δὲ τὸν χρόνον ἐκεῖνον, κ α ὶ συμμαχικὸν ἔπεμψε Καίσαρι πεντακοσίους ἐπιλέκτους τῶν σωματοφυλάκων, οὓς Γάλλος Αἴλιος περὶ τὴν Ἐρυθρὰν Ͽάλασσαν ἦγεν.

from the head of the Red Sea. But here it was found[1] that the ships built for the expedition were unsuited by their size and draught for the shallows they would have to encounter, and new vessels had to be constructed, which caused a delay till the spring of 23. Arriving at Leuce-Come in Arabia, the force was kept there all that summer and winter by sickness,[2] and it was not till the close of 22, at least nine months after starting out in the spring, that they returned, a scanty remnant, ingloriously to Alexandria.[3] In the meantime,[4] as Strabo proceeds to relate,[4] the Ethiopians, taking advantage of the diminished forces in Egypt, drawn off by Gallus in his expedition, descended the Nile and plundered the towns about the first cataract. The prefect Petronius marched with less than ten thousand foot and eight hundred horse against them, drove them back, and pursued them to Pselchis; thence he advanced to Premnis, and even captured and destroyed Napata, the capital of Queen Candace. Then he returned to Alexandria with his booty and prisoners, one thousand of whom he sent to Augustus, "lately"[5] returned from the Cantabri (Spain). The Ethiopians were not content with their first defeat, but again attacked the Roman outpost at Premnis.[6] Petronius marched a second time to meet them, and succeeded in throwing his forces into Premnis before the enemy had captured it. They were glad to send him an embassy, which he would not answer in person, but despatched to the emperor, *whom they found in Samos on his way to Syria.* He had remained at Rome till the fall of 22; then he had set out for Sicily while, as Dio says,[7] the events just narrated were taking place in Egypt. He spent the winter of 22–21 in Sicily, and had thence visited Sparta and other Greek towns, arriving in Samos in the winter of 21–20.[8]

Here, then, we have Petronius traced as prefect of Egypt at least from 25 to 20 B.C. Consequently, *Barbarus could not have been prefect in 23–22 by any possibility.* It is supposed by many that Ælius Gallus succeeded Petronius about the year 20; but how long

---

[1] Strabo, 780.   [2] Strabo, 781.   [3] Strabo, 782.

[4] I. e., in the year 22, according to Dio, liv. 5.   [5] Strabo, 820, 821.

[4] νεωστί, a very indefinite word, which will not admit of any exact limitation.

[7] Strabo, 821.   [6] liv. 6.   [8] Dio, liv. 7; Josephus, Antiq. Jud. xv. 10, 3.

he held the post, or who were his successors till the time of Æmilius
Rectus, A.D. 14, our ancient authorities do not tell us, except so far
as to mention the names of Aquila and Maximus, who are supposed
to fall somewhere within this interval. It was left to inscriptions to
supply all the additional information we have, and those in the
"Corpus" give us only Turranius in B.C. 7, and Octavius A.D. 1.

When I had arrived at this point in the investigation, and found
that my own conclusions, based upon these ancient authors, were
supported by Letronne, Franz, and Merivale, I was greatly puzzled
by the inscription. Archæology must go hand in hand with history;
at least she must not, in a moment of frenzy, dash her brains out
against a solid wall of established facts. Where, then, was the key
to all these contradictions and inconsistencies? I visited the Museum
for a second time February 6th, and tried to extract something from
the Latin. Advance was made only so far as to note some marks
before CAESARIS with a straight line over them, that might indicate
a number in Roman characters; and I reached the gratifying result
that the letter before the second A in the line below might be S, G, R,
or B, its predecessor looking more like X than anything else! Furthermore, that a Greek letter, Ψ, was to be seen in the upper left-hand
corner of the Latin inscription, standing alone by itself, and cut at a
somewhat different angle from the letters of the Latin.

February 9th I made a third visit late in the afternoon in company with Dr. E. D. Perry. When we arrived, Mr. W. C. Prime had
just left the Museum, after making a careful examination of the
inscriptions, and General Cesnola directed our attention to what
Mr. Prime now thought were traces of something resembling I in the
Greek before the H of the date. Both Dr. Perry and myself declared
at once that this was an indisputable fact, as we traced the outlines
down, and I remembered then to have noticed these tracings on my
second visit, but my attention being called away at the moment, they
had gone quite out of my memory. This vertical mark lay directly
at the base and close under the projecting knob of the crab, so that
it was partly shaded by it, and not easily discerned except from a
proper position, since the cut was filled quite to the surface with
oxidation. I immediately hailed the discovery as the probable

solution of the main difficulties of the problem. The key had fallen quite unexpectedly into our hands; for the character was a Greek iota, which, prefixed to the II, altered the date ten years, and brought it down to B.C. 13–12, which I knew to be somewhere near the date of an inscription from Philæ, published by Wescher, and containing the name of P. Rubrius Barbarus, as mentioned in a note by Mr. G. L. Feuardent in Commander Gorringe's "Obelisks." Accordingly, the next thing was to find this inscription and ascertain its exact form and purport. But first I obtained a promise from General Cesnola that he would have the oxidation removed next day from the iota, since it was so important that there should be no possible doubt about the existence and form of this letter. I had said to him while examining the inscriptions for the first time, that it was impossible to read them with any approach to scientific exactness, without the removal of the oxidation and other accumulation which filled and obscured so many of the lines. Upon his assurance that this could be done without injury to the bronze (as, indeed, the result proved), I now urged it still more strongly, and went early next morning to Mr. Prime, who is a trustee of the Museum, to obtain his consent to the cleaning process, which he kindly gave me.[1] I then called upon Mr. Feuardent to obtain such information as he could give me towards finding the Wescher inscription, and told him of the discovery of the iota and the proposed removal of the oxidation that day. Hastening to the Astor Library, I entered upon a long hunt for the article, in which I was obligingly assisted by the librarians, but without success, in consequence of the unfamiliar form of the citation; and the search was on the point of being abandoned for the time when, upon the reference being laid before the Superintendent, he at once recognized the work and handed me the volume, "Bullettino dell' Instituto di Corrispondenza Archeologica," 1866. Here was the article in question, pp. 44–56, and the inscription ran thus:

ΑΥΤΟΚΡΑΤΟΡΙΚΑΙΣΑΡΙΣΕΒΑΣΤΩΙΣΩΤΗΡΙΚΑΙΕΥΕΡΓΕΤΗΙ.ΙΗ
ΕΠΙΠΟΠΛΙΟΥΡΟΒΡΙΟΥΒΑΡΒΑΡΟΥ

---

[1] That all scruples were needless may be seen by consulting foot-note, p. 39. It was supposed, at this time, however, that the condition of the bronze was the same as when originally unearthed.

2

" To the Emperor Cæsar, the August, the Saviour and Benefactor, in the 18th year. Under the auspices of Publius Rubrius Barbarus."[1] This inscription was discovered by Wescher while attached to the mission of M. de Rougé, 1863–64, on a visit to Philæ in company with Mariette-Bey. It was found on an architrave of gray granite close to the ruins of a structure of the Roman period of the Doric order. The architrave was three and a half metres long by half a metre high, the letters large and well formed, measuring on an average sixty-five millimetres in height.

Here, then, is the full name of our Barbarus, and not only is the date precisely the same as that of the crab, but the two inscriptions also harmonize epigraphically in the form of the crucial A and Σ. Two considerable works, then, were executed in the same year—the erection of the obelisks at Alexandria, and the construction and dedication of this building (probably a temple) at Philæ to the emperor. In the first instance, Barbarus declares that he performed the task himself (of course through his architect); in the other, it was done "under his auspices." The prefect had his seat of government in Alexandria, and only occasionally made a tour through the province. Philæ, the holy isle, where statues had been erected to the emperor as early as the time of Petronius,[2] was at the other extremity of Egypt, on the very confines of Ethiopia, nearly seven hundred miles up the Nile. I say "our Barbarus," and include him among the prefects; for I had now no hesitation in asserting him to be the prefect of Egypt in B.C. 13–12, a date removed from all historical objections. Wescher (and of course Mariette, who was with him), F. Feuardent ("Numismatique de l'Égypte Ancienne"), and Boutkowski ("Dictionnaire Numismatique," 1881) were satisfied to denominate him prefect on the authority of the Philæ inscription alone; we now have still more convincing proof. The argument is this:

In administering the affairs of Egypt as a province the Romans divided the country into three great districts, the Thebais on the south, the Heptanomis in the central part, and the Delta, or lower

---

[1] In Greek inscriptions before our era, O is the regular representative of the Latin U in proper names, and Poplius is in fact the elder Latin form for Publius.

[2] Strabo, 820.

Egypt, on the north. In addition to these, the earlier division into subdistricts or Nomes, of which Strabo tells us there were thirty-six at this time, was allowed to remain. The prefect was supreme ruler over the entire province. Over each of the three great divisions presided an officer called Epistrategus, who was habitually a Roman, chosen from the train of the prefect; but over each Nome was a native Greek called Strategus. From the inscriptions we perceive that when a dedication was inscribed it was usual to add the name of one or more of these magistrates, often of all three, the Prefect, the Epistrategus of the district where the dedication was made, and the Strategus of the Nome. As for instance, in C. I. 4715, by which alone we are informed that Publius Octavius was prefect A.D. 1, we read that "The people of the city Tentyris and of the Nome dedicate to Isis and the associate gods the propylon of the temple in behalf of the Emperor Cæsar, the son of the god, Zeus the Liberator, the August, under Publius Octavius, Prefect, and Marcus Clodius Postumus, Epistrategus, Tryphon, Strategus."[1] As here, the names and titles are generally given, preceded by the preposition ΕΠΙ, with the meaning, "in the time of," "under the auspices of." Now, our Philae inscription fails directly to style Barbarus prefect, in the same manner as the Greek of the crab, nor is any other title given him. But if he had been Strategus of the Nome at Philae, his name would not have been a Latin one. Likewise, he would not have been Epistrategus of the Thebais, and had anything to do with the monument at Alexandria in the same year. Consequently, the two inscriptions, coming from the opposite confines of the province, and engraved upon such important memorials in the same year, must refer to the officer whose power extended over the entire country, namely, the prefect and the prefect only.

On the evening of the same 10th of February, while examining a very carefully prepared lead impression of the Latin of the crab, I noticed, while tracing back the marks to the left of CAESARIS, that there was a short one which did not run vertically like the rest, but diverged

---

[1] Ὑπὲρ Αὐτοκράτορος Καίσαρος, θεοῦ υἱοῦ, Διὸς Ἐλευθερίου, Σεβαστοῦ, ἐπὶ Ποπλίου Ὀκταυίου ἡγεμόνος καὶ Μάρκου Κλωδίου Ποστόμου ἐπιστρατήγου, Τρύφωνος στρατηγοῦντος, οἱ ἀπὸ τῆς μητροπόλεως καὶ τοῦ νομοῦ τὸ πρόπυλον Ἴσιδι θεᾷ μεγίστῃ καὶ τοῖς συννάοις θεοῖς ἔτους λα Καίσαρος, Θωὺθ Σεβαστῇ.

at a distinct angle to the others until it came to a deep cut and was lost. This, I thought, might be the right limb of a v, and so traced that letter out on paper in the same angular proportion. Then passing on over the surface ruined by cuts, a faintly outlined O revealed itself, and adjacent to this a very plain upright cut which traced out into an N. Next, after a space, came a fair A with some marks of N between. Adding these to my paper, I found that the space between O and the supposed V would just contain an X of the same proportions as the adjacent letters. As all the other words in the several lines are written without spaces between to divide them, I inserted the X and read ANNOXVIIICAESARIS, for the first line of the Latin, which then corresponded exactly to the first line of the Greek, date and all.[1] Hence the inference was irresistible that, as both the Greek and Latin harmonized at the close, and probably harmonized at the beginning, and Barbarus must have been prefect in that year, BARBARVS was the name which originally stood before PRAEF, whatever was to be found there now.

Here we have arrived at a point where some additional testimony may properly be brought to bear. Pliny (xxxvi. 14), writing not later than 78 A.D., states that the pair of obelisks, of which ours is one, were standing before the Cæsareum in his time. Now, no Cæsars reigned eighteen years up to 78 A.D., except Augustus and Tiberius; hence the erection by Barbarus must be limited to these two reigns at most. But the prefects of the reign of Tiberius are all known and their years accounted for (C. I. iii. p. 310). Therefore the prefecture of Barbarus must fall into the period between B.C. 20 and A.D. 14, in the reign of Augustus.

On Monday the 12th I visited the Museum again, and found that the removal of the oxidation from the iota had disclosed the original

---

[1] These additions, as well as those afterwards obtained by the cleaning process, in both Greek and Latin, are indicated in the fac-similes (b) (b). The X of this date is almost entirely ruined by the injury above, but some slight indications of the lower limb on the left I have ventured to mark. I am glad to add to my own observation the testimony of Professor Isaac H. Hall, who was an early disbeliever in the correctness of the inscriptions as published. Upon a recent visit to the city he made a careful examination of the bronze, and writes me under date of May 7th, "Before CAESARIS the first line has unmistakable traces of ANNO XVIII."

letter as deeply, clearly, and regularly cut as any in the line, and I was able to verify from the bronze all that I had recently discovered in the Latin date. I took also a very careful transcript of everything I could make out along the line where BARBARVS ought to stand, preparatory to the continuance of the cleaning process, at which I had arranged to be present on the following day while the repairer of the Museum was engaged in the work. This arrangement was carried out on the 13th, and after some time devoted to clearing out the Σ and the following A of KAIΣAP, and the Σ of BAPBAPOΣ in the Greek, we turned our attention to the desperate ʢ at the beginning of the second line of the Latin. Here, slowly and gradually, as the cuts were traced out and cleared of the oxidation, a well-formed B disclosed itself, the upper part having been so completely closed that not a single trace had appeared before the process began. The curved appendage to the right still remained, but the original B is distinct enough, although the oxidation was not wholly removed from the upper curve. Preceding the B a cut was found, but it did not seem to form itself into any kind of a letter; it resembles rather the external mark beyond POSVIT. A few moments devoted to the space on the left of the second A revealed the lower half of a B pretty clearly. At this stage the process was suspended till a later day.

On the afternoon of the 17th, you will remember, Sir, that you met me at the Museum, in order that ocular evidence might be added to your previous examination of the drawings and squeezes, and we went carefully over the whole ground of both inscriptions.

On the 22d the process of cleaning was again resumed in my presence, beginning with the now less dubious BARBARVS of the Latin. Little appeared at the time to be gained from the letter after the first A, and it was not till I had brought under the microscope a lead squeeze taken after we had finished for the day, that I observed that one of the marks in the upper limb to the right, which I supposed to be straight, has actually a very definite curve, as would be proper for an R. This can now be seen on the bronze with the naked eye, and renders the R certain, though the major part of the letter has nearly disappeared, and the whole surface in this vicinity is considerably marred. The next letter became somewhat more plainly a B, with an

extraneous cut running obliquely quite across it.   The lower part of
this had been visible before, and gave rise to the supposition that the
letter was more likely to be R than B.   Passing over the adjacent A,
which is plain enough, we took up the stumbling-block F, with the
mark to the right which at first sight appears to run up as far as the
left limb of the V and form therewith an irregular N.   Close inspec-
tion of the bronze, however, and of a squeeze under the microscope,
shows that it does not connect with the V, and, in fact, that there is a
break between the deep cut at the bottom and the slighter incision
higher up.   Removal of the incrustation rendered more apparent a
depression running from this deep cut at the right with something of
a curve up to the middle mark of the F, with some slight indications
of its continuance round again to the right towards the top of the
letter; but there the furrow from the extraneous gouge above has
been pressed down over the surface quite to the top of the F, and
forms a high ridge, extending from the perpendicular cut through to
the V, but leaves the perpendicular uncovered, so that this is seen
originally to have continued somewhat higher, till it reached a point
parallel with the apex of the adjacent A, *which the F does not do.*
This leads me to believe that the top of the original R is covered up
by the overlapping furrow, as is the case with the extremity of the
right limb of the V and the top of the S; and that the upper limb of
the F is a more recent attempt of some one, at an unknown period,
possibly to restore what he mistook from the faintness of the original,
or purposely to mislead.   Other evidences of tampering with this
word are plain, so that it offers a fertile field for a plentiful crop of
conjectures.   The second A exhibits several random cuts on the
right limb; and it seems to me likely that the appendages of the first
B and A and the F must be laid at the door of the ancient attempt to
mislead.   However this may be, the cross to the left of AEGYPTI, which
is slightly but plainly cut, is evidence of later treatment, at all events.[1]

---

[1] The Greek cross within the H of the Greek date, if a genuine cut, is something similar, but this seems rather a series of fortuitous **breaks** in the surface-crust, which is here
quite thick, and it is plainly no more than a mere scratch in the bronze at the best.
Still, it is not unnatural that some zealous Christian should have utilized the bronze
for engraving this symbol, after the heathen gods had been ejected from the temple,
especially as IH were the first letters of IHΣOYΣ.

The supposition that the prefect's name here was purposely destroyed or erased by some successor, or by the order of the emperor (cases of which are not rare), is disproved by the fact that the name was allowed to remain quite uninjured on the more conspicuous side of the claw and in the far more conspicuous letters of the Greek. It may be urged that the incision, which seems to me to be connected with the F to form the original R, is out of proportion for that letter; but an examination of the other R's of the inscription will prove that this wide extension at the bottom is a peculiarity of all of them. But about this letter in particular there is much room for difference of opinion, though it is plain that BARBARVS must be read here.

Passing to the line above, the Greek Ψ was cleared out in part, and something, though not much, was done to the date to the right. Here, whatever had not been destroyed by the injuries came out with greater distinctness, especially the horizontal line over the XVIII. Some marks in the upper corner of the bronze, over CAESARIS, were examined, but they did not shape themselves into letters. At this stage the work was suspended.

Some minor points of the inscriptions may now be considered. ΑΝΕΘΗΚΕ of the Greek is sometimes used in the sense of "consecrating," sometimes of "setting up" simply. In the former case, it usually has the object of consecration expressed in the dative case; but C. I. 4684b is an example, among others, where this is omitted altogether. For its employment in relation to obelisks, we have the authority of Herodotus (ii. 111), where he says that two obelisks were erected and consecrated by King Pheros at the Temple of the Sun in Heliopolis. In like manner Pliny (xxxvi. 14) uses POSVIT when speaking of an obelisk erected by Rameses in the same city.

The published ΑΡΧΙΤΕΚΤΟΝ ΟΥΝΤΟΣ is, of course, an impossibility for ΑΡΧΙΤΕΚΤΟΝΟΥΝΤΟΣ, as it is written on the bronze. The expression is employed just as in Plutarch (Pericl. 13), where he says that "the Propylæa of the Acropolis was completed within the space of five years, Μνησικλέους ἀρχιτεκτονοῦντος." Similarly, C. I. 4897d. For the use of the noun ΑΡΧΙΤΕΚΤΩΝ, of one who superintends the transportation of these huge masses of stone, we have again the authority of Herodotus (ii. 175), when describing the conveyance of an enormous monolithic chapel from Elephantine to Sais in the time of Amasis.

The X of ΑΡΧΙΤΕΚΤΟΝΟΥΝΤΟΣ appears at first sight no more than half made; but this is simply due to the oxidation which has closed up the lower part of both branches, and the outline of the one on the left can be easily traced.[1]

On the opposite side of the bronze it seems doubtful if the E of AEGYPTI was ever cut in full; some depressions about the lower part do not appear to be connected with the small E above. The character Υ is the Greek, not the Latin, form of the letter, and similarly the ΓΙ for PT is a common form on the coins of the Ptolemies, often employed there as the monogram of the name of those kings. This led me at the outset to suppose that the engraver was a Greek, as, indeed, would accord naturally with the circumstances of the day at Alexandria, and might explain the apparent addition to the final I of the word, if it is a genuine original cut. The three letters last engraved having been Greek, the workman had unconsciously begun the next letter with the form of the Greek genitive case, ΑΙΓΥΠΤΟΥ, in his mind, and nearly formed an O before he discovered his error. Then he corrected it as far as possible by his very substantial I. Some such confusion appears to be visible also in the final letter of ARCHITECTANTE. With these circumstances I connect the presence of the Greek Ψ in the upper corner on this inside face, since it may well be the initial of the engraver.

An example of the combination of the repeated N we have upon the coin of M. Lepidus, which he had struck to commemorate his appointment by the Roman Senate as guardian of the youthful Ptolemy Epiphanes (B.C. 204–180): S.C.TVTOR.REG. M.LEPIDVS.PON.MAX.

For the expression ANNOXVIIICAESARIS, we have a parallel, engraved by a later prefect, on the so-called vocal statue of Memnon at Thebes, as follows: ANNO.VII.IMP.CAESARIS.NERVAE.TRAIANI. AUG.GER.DACICI.C.VIBIVS.MAXIMVS.PRAEF.AEG.AVDIT.MEMNONEM. XIIII.K.MAR.HORA.IIS.SEMEL.III.SEM.

The pages of ancient writers are totally and provokingly silent concerning Publius Rubrius Barbarus, though in this he has shared

---

a common fate with the two prefects who followed him, Turranius, B.C. 7,[1] and Octavius, A.D. 1, who are certainly known to us only through a single inscription each. The Rubrian family was of plebeian origin, and attained to equestrian rank, but never played any very important part in history. The first appearance of the name is in connection with the reforms of Tiberius Gracchus, B.C. 133. Some Rubrius was tribune of the people, and presided at the election for the coming year; and, though the friend of Gracchus, he did not act with sufficient firmness at a critical moment, and the death of his colleague was the result.[2]

Again, a Rubrius is mentioned by Plutarch[2] as tribune, a colleague and supporter of Caius Gracchus. He brought forward, in the interest of Gracchus, a proposal known as the Rubrian law, for the colonization of Carthage, B.C. 123.

Historians have clearly shown how the principles of the Gracchi were handed down through Marius to Julius Cæsar till they culminated in the empire, and that a regular succession is to be found in what may be termed the Gracchan-Marian-Cæsarian party. We find the Rubrii attached to this party at the outset, and it is a noticeable circumstance that this attachment seems to have been continued with unusual fidelity, except under the influence of Cato, in B.C. 49. In the Marian troubles Q. Rubrius Varro was adjudged an enemy to the state by the Senate, along with Marius himself, in B.C. 88. Cicero describes him as a sharp and vehement prosecutor.[3]

L. Rubrius Dossenus was master of the mint, and struck numerous coins between 87 and 81 B.C. Their date is determined by the nature of the find at Montecodruzzo.

Cicero mentions[4] a Rubrius in the train of Verres at Lampsacus, and gives him a rather bad character. Of Publius and Quintus Rubrius, who were in Sicily under Verres about 70 B.C., Cicero speaks in more flattering language.[5]

---

[1] This date, though left somewhat in doubt by the "Corpus," is now fixed by Wescher, who examined it carefully when at Philæ.

[2] Appian, Bel. Civil. i. 14. [3] C. Gracch. x. [4] Brut. 45.

[5] In Verr. i. 25. [4] In Verr. iii. 57, 80.

An inscription from Capua mentions Aulus Rubrius, son of Aulus, B.C. 71.[1] Another still earlier, B.C. 104, speaks of N. Rubrius, son of Marcus, at the same place.[2]

M. Rubrius was pretor in Macedonia about 67 B.C., and under him the younger Cato served as military tribune.[3]

Cicero mentions a Rubria who was the mother of his friend Carbo.[4]

L. Rubrius, a senator, joined the party of Pompey when Cæsar was crossing the Rubicon, and so many were of two minds, was taken prisoner at Corfinium and pardoned on the spot, B.C. 49.[5]

Within the same year, or soon after, some Rubrius, as tribune of the people, according to Mommsen,[6] brought forward the law known as the Rubrian, relating to citizenship in Cisalpine Gaul. This was done in the interest, and at the dictation, of Cæsar.

M. Rubrius, who was with Cato in Utica, B.C. 46, I take to be the one above mentioned as Cato's old commander in Macedonia.[7]

About this time is to be placed the L. Rubrius of Casinum, who made Antony his heir, passing over his own nephew, although he had never seen Antony, and did not know whether he was black or white, as Cicero says, in his Philippic strain.[8]

An actor named Rubrius resembled so closely the orator Plancus, Pliny tells us,[9] that he obtained his surname from him.

Rubrius Rex, or Ruga, is named by Appian[10] as one of the assassins of Cæsar. Nicolaus of Damascus[11] adds that Minucius, while striking at the Dictator with his dagger, wounded Rubrius in the thigh.

Next comes an inscription[12] originally read by Muratori towards the beginning of the last century at Monte Casino, the ancient Casinum. It declares that P. Rubrius M. F. MAELARBA dedicates some monument to Augustus in B.C. 21.[13]

[1] Orelli, 6119.
[2] Plut. Cato Min. 9; Drumann, Gesch. v. p. 154.
[3] Caes. Bel. Civil. 23.
[4] Plut. Cato Min. 62.
[5] Bel. Civil. ii. 113.
[6] Wilm. No. 2018.
[7] Epist. ad Fam. ix. 21.
[8] C. I. L. i. p. 118; Hermes, 1881, 1.
[9] Phil. ii. 16.
[10] Nat. Hist. vii. 10.
[11] Vit. Aug.
[12] Orelli, No. 597.

[13]   IMP. CAESARI
DIVI. F. AVGVSTO
COS. XI. IMP. VIII.
TRIBVNIC. POTESTAT. III.
P. RVBRIVS. M. F. MAELARBA.

P. Rubrius BARBARVS is prefect of Egypt, B.C. 13-12.

An inscription[1] informs us that Rubria Ichmas (a freedwoman of the Rubrian family) was nurse of Quinta, daughter of Barbarus. She died at the age of fifty, and her memorial was erected by Daphnus, the butler of T. Rubrius Nepos.

Another inscription[2] says that T. Rubrius Nepos was curator of aqueducts with A. Didius Gallus and M. Cornelius Firmus, of whom Didius Gallus is mentioned by Frontinus as holding this office from A.D. 39 to 49.

In the reign of Augustus an impostor attempted to palm herself off as a real Rubria who was supposed to have perished in a conflagration at Mediolanum; but the emperor refused to admit her into the gens, though supported by numerous witnesses of the place, and by the " Augustan cohort," and finally she was compelled to retire baffled.[3]

An inscription[4] gives us another native of Casinum, M. Rubrius Proculus, who was an Augustalis or priest of the deified Augustus.

Rubrius, a Roman knight, was accused before Tiberius of violating the name of the deified Augustus by perjury. Tiberius treated the case lightly, and declared that the gods could take care of such cases themselves.[5]

Rubrius Fabatus was arrested in flight to the Parthians, A.D. 32, but received no punishment.[6]

Rubrius Pollio was in high favor with Claudius on his return from Britain, A.D. 44.[7]

One of the family was a vestal virgin maltreated by Nero,[8] and another a court physician, noted for the extravagant fees he received.[9]

Rubrius Gallus was sent by Nero, A.D. 68, against Galba, after his revolt;[10] and a Rubrius Gallus was consul A.D. 101. This appears to have been the highest post to which any of the family attained at Rome. I have gathered a large number of inscriptions in which the name occurs, in various parts of Italy, Spain, Dalmatia, Pannonia, Greece, Asia Minor, and Africa, but little is to be extracted from

[1] C. I. L. vi. 9245. [2] C. I. L. vi. 1248. [3] Val. Max. ix. 15.
[4] Muratori, 1036, 6. [5] Tac. An. i. 73. [6] Tac. An. vi. 14.
[7] Dio, lx. 23. [8] Suet. Nero, 28. [9] Pliny, xxix. 5.
[10] Dio, lxiii. 27.

the bare list, especially as few are dated; but there are two which re-
veal more than inscriptions usually do. At Brixia, as it appears,
lived P. Rubrius Celer, who erected a memorial to his dear and loving
wife, with whom he had lived forty-three years and eight months *sine
querela*, without a single complaint. T. Rubrius lived at Rome for
seventy-five years and taught for fifty.

The object in collecting the series of Rubrii above was, of course,
to glean what information was possible touching our prefect. In
piecing together such disconnected accounts, one must needs run
some hazard; but a certain combination has seemed to me possible,
and I venture to advance it with the proviso that it is subject to re-
vision or complete rejection, like any other tentative conjecture. It
is based, in the first place, upon the belief that P. Rubrius MAE-
LARBA, who dedicated the monument at Casinum to Augustus,
B.C. 21, is in reality P. Rubrius BARBARVS, MAELARBA being either a
misreading for BARBARVS on a stone somewhat defaced or incrusted
by time (BARBARVS of the crab having been quite as desperate before it was cleaned), or else a misreading in some other way for the
same. The name MAELARBA seems unprecedented; at all events,
I have hunted for it through many myriads of Roman names in
ancient authors and inscriptions, and have yet to find a single
instance of its recurrence. Furthermore, the name of Muratori,
who first copied the inscription (220, 8, "*e schedis meis*"), is almost a
by-word among men of that craft, not only for carelessness, but for
arbitrary changes which he introduced into his readings; so that of
his fifteen thousand inscriptions more than one thousand have been
given in an emended form by his more painstaking and accurate
successors in that department of study. I conceive, then, that in a
hurried hour Muratori transcribed the inscription accurately enough
in the important part relating to Augustus, but the last word after
an insignificant name he did not take the trouble to decipher with
care, but wrote down what the letters seemed to him most nearly to
resemble, since he gives us no hint of any mutilation of the monument. If the stone is still in existence to disprove this theory, I
shall hasten to offer my heartiest apologies to the memory of the
good Muratori for slandering him; but I have not yet been able to

ascertain that it has been read by any other editor. It is quite possible that it now rests among the treasures of the old Benedictine monastery at Monte Casino, among the Sabine hills southeast of Rome, and I have written to W. Henzen, First Secretary to the Imperial Archæological Institute of Germany, and one of the editors of the Roman inscriptions now publishing, and I hope soon to have some more accurate information in relation to it.

That this P. Rubrius of Casinum is a zealous partisan of Augustus in B.C. 21 is plain from the inscription, and he is here engaged in doing on a smaller scale what the grander prefect of Egypt did later on at Philæ. Furthermore, he is the son of Marcus—perhaps the very Marcus who was the pretor in Macedonia and the friend of Cato; perhaps, too, the nephew of L. Rubrius of Casinum, who is brought into relation with Cæsar or Augustus and his followers by the bequeathal of his property to Antony, passing over his nephew, who could take care of himself, or might even be furthered in his career by such action of the uncle. Again, the mover of the Rubrian law in 49 must have been a trusty adherent of Cæsar to have been selected by him among his colleagues for that important duty; and conceiving this to have been his first entrance into public life as tribune of the people, at about thirty years, P. Rubrius would be of a fitting age in B.C. 13–12 for the responsible duties of Egyptian prefect, and to be numbered in that series of "sober and discreet men," as Strabo calls them,[1] who succeeded each other in that important office. At all events, some such career as this just outlined he must needs have followed, to attain a position which was almost the equal of kings; and, according to the policy of Augustus, laid down at the outset in relation to that post, he must have been of equestrian rank and a favored and favorite partisan of the emperor himself. His cognomen Barbarus may have been won in some campaigns in which he distinguished himself against the enemies of Rome, or it may have been given him by his father in commemoration of some of his own exploits. He was evidently proud of it, selecting it alone, as he did, to perpetuate himself on the great monument of the obelisk. It is not a very common appellation, but we find an Atilius Barbarus who was

---

[1] Strabo, 797.

consul in A.D. 72, and M. Civica Barbarus consul A.D. 157. A few others might be cited from the inscriptions, but they are few, as I have said.

If the Barbarus mentioned above, whose daughter Quinta was nursed by Rubria Ichmas, is to be identified with our Barbarus, as seems possible, we have a bit of family history, to the effect that he was the father of five daughters. When the prefect returned from Egypt he would naturally have been accompanied by a large train of slaves whom he had gathered about him in his almost regal state. Many of these would become manumitted for their fidelity, ability, or other cause, and would then, as was the custom, take the prenomen and gentile name of their master, together with a specific cognomen of their own, usually that by which they had been known before. The close connection between our Rubrius and the emperor is again exhibited by the fact that a number of these freedmen became attached to the house of Augustus, and their memorials are found in the columbaria or vaults where such retainers of the imperial family were buried. One of these columbaria, discovered in 1852 on the Appian Way near the tomb of the Scipios, and containing the names of Augustus, Tiberius, Julia, and Germanicus, also disclosed the following list of Rubrian liberti: P. Rubrius, Rubria;[1] P. Rubrius Abascantus, Rubria Lexis, P. Rubrius Polybius;[2] P. Rubrius Anicetus, Rubria Thallusa;[3] P. Rubrius Hilarus, Rubria Glymene;[4] P. Rubrius Gatis, P. Rubrius P. . . . ;[5] P. Rubrius Hilarus, Rubria Aprodisia, freedwoman of Publius;[6] P. Rubrius Priscus, Rubria Hermais;[7] Rubria Veneria, P. Rubrius Myrsinus, Rubria Galene.[8] Another similar columbarium, found near the Porta Latina in 1831, contains the name of P. Rubrius Epaphroditus.[9]

Such are the meagre details which may be patched up from the *disjecta membra* of antiquity in relation to this family, which has become so interesting a one to us through the erection of our obelisk at Alexandria by one of its members, and the re-erection of the same here in our midst, and our possession of the memorial which he had

---

[1] C. I. L. vi. 5284. [2] Ibid. 5334. [3] Ibid. 5335.
[4] Ibid. 5336. [5] Ibid. 5346. [6] Ibid. 5465.
[7] Ibid. 5466. [8] Ibid. 5467. [9] Ibid. 5616.

inscribed to his own honor as well as to that of his beloved Cæsar. What further light may be thrown upon the family by inscriptions discovered and not yet published, or yet to be discovered, is left for the future to disclose.

The foregoing had been written and submitted, as you will remember, Sir, to yourself, Professor Drisler, and others, as early as the 15th of March. On the 2d of April, in answer to my letter to Dr. Henzen, a reply was received, from which the following is extracted:

" In my opinion, it is most probable that the inscription of Casinum, Orelli, 597, belongs to your prefect; you may find the right reading in Mommsen's ' Inscrip. Regni Neapol.' 4229, and will find it in a few weeks in the C. I. L. x. No. 5169, that volume being almost ready to appear. The true text of the inscription is this:

IMP. CAESARI. DIVI. F
AVGVSTO
COS. XI. IMP. VII
TRIBVNIC. POTESTAt
P. RVBRIVS. M. F. MAE. BARBArus

It has been copied by Brunn, and Mommsen himself. Brunn believed that he saw part of a T at the end of the last line, and Mommsen, in the C. I. L., supplies BARBAtus; but I think there may have been vestiges of the vertical line that may have belonged as well to an R as to a T."

My conjecture, then, is happily confirmed in this particular, and the connection of the other Rubrii at Casinum is greatly strengthened, while this town is proved to have been the seat of that branch of the Rubrian family to which Barbarus belonged.

Obtaining access to the " Inscrip. Regni Neapol." of Mommsen, referred to by Dr. Henzen, I find the following note upon the readings of the last line of the inscription: "MAE. P, Ambr. sched.; MAELARBA, frater; MAELARBA, reliqui; dedi conjecturam (MAE. BARBA) Kellermanni." It will be observed that in the third line IMP. VII is now read for the IMP. VIII of Muratori, and in the fourth line TRIBUNIC.POTESTA for his TRIBUNIC.POTEST.III. This leaves the question of date somewhat in doubt. Augustus was COS. XI in B.C. 23, but retained the same title for seventeen years.[1] He is known to have been styled IMP. VII in B.C. 29, and Eckhel supposed that he had fixed the limit of its use by this inscription of Casinum as read by Muratori; but this is now left doubtful. We find, however, the title IMP. VIII on coins assigned to B.C. 20,[2] and IMP. IX in the year 19.[3] The Tribunician power in perpetuity was bestowed on the emperor in the year 23, probably on the 27th of June, and it was numbered annually from that date on to his death. The probability is, therefore, that our inscription falls into the years 23–22, or not long after, certainly not later than 20.

The slab upon which this inscription was found is described as a particolored marble, engraved with very beautiful letters, and still preserved among the antiquities at Monte Casino. Muratori undoubtedly did copy in haste, and took no account of the injury which the slab had received upon the right side. "MAE." is an abbreviation for MAECIA, the tribe to which Barbarus belonged. Such addition to a proper name is frequent in inscriptions and legal documents.

Somewhat later in the day on the 2d of April I received another letter from Dr. Henzen, as follows:

"When I wrote you the other day, I forgot to tell you that the inscription of your obelisk has been amply illustrated by Professor Lumbroso in the Bullettino of the Institute, 1878, p. 54, and by Mommsen, ' Ephem. Epigr.' iv. p. 27. You will find there all we may know about that prefect, except the inscription of Casinum, which you very probably refer to him."

This seemed to portend that much of my work had been anticipated. At all events, the correctness of the inscription would be challenged on the ground of the impossibility of the prefecture of Barbarus falling in the year 23–22, when Strabo says that Petronius was prefect. Hastening to the Bullettino for 1878 I found the article of Professor Lumbroso, from which I translate the substance:

"In the ' Bulletin de correspondance hellenique,' December 1,

---

[1] Suet. Aug. 26.   [2] Cohen, Descrip. Monn. No. 79.   [3] Cohen, Nos. 37, 40.

1877, there is related the notable discovery in Alexandria on the 20th of June, 1877, of a bilingual inscription in Greek and Latin, which was read by Mr. Neroutsos, upon the right claw of the mutilated crab found under the standing obelisk.   It reads as follows:

L H ΚΑΙΣΑΡΟΣ
ΒΑΡΒΑΡΟΣ ΑΝΕΘΗΚΕ
ΑΡΧΙΤΕΚΤΟΝΟΥΝΤΟΣ
ΠΟΝΤΙΟΥ

ANNO VIII
AVGVSTI CAESARIS
BARBARVS PRAEF.
AEGYPTI POSVIT
ARCHITECTANTE PONTIO

" Wescher published in the Bullettino for 1866 a fac-simile of an inscription from Philæ, dedicated by the prefect of Egypt, P. Rubrius Barbarus, in the eighteenth year of Augustus (see above, p. 19), in which it will be observed that the I adscript of ΕΥΕΡΓΕΤΗ is not written, as it is in the preceding word ΣΕΒΑΣΤΩΙ, a fact which Wescher has not noticed.   As this is an anomaly, though not without precedent, the suspicion arises that this I ought to be found in the vertical limb of the L (ΕΥΕΡΓΕΤΗΙ.ΙΗ), while the following I of the inscription is really the L or symbol for the year ; consequently, the Philæ inscription and that of the crab belong to one and the same year, and the lacuna which the series of prefects of Egypt presents is now filled in the eighth year of Augustus."

This seems harsh treatment for an inscription whose letters are " large and well formed," and read by two very careful archæologists, Wescher and Mariette-Bey, to say nothing of the fact that Barbarus is now proved by the inscription from Casinum to have been quietly at home in that " noteworthy town," as Strabo calls it, at about the time that he is made prefect of Egypt by Lumbroso.

But, at all events, we are getting back to the origin of the errors in our inscription as published here.   Lumbroso has copied it from Neroutsos, and when his version is compared with that with which we began at the very outset, it will be seen that they differ in two particulars only.   ANNO is no longer written, as by Neroutsos, with broken lines,' as doubtful or supplied from the Greek, and ΑΡΧΙΤΕΚΤΟΝΟΥΝΤΟΣ has become ΑΡΧΙΤΕΚΤΟΝ ΟΥΝΤΟΣ.   In both,

---

' I find later that both in the Alexandrian paper, as copied by Mommsen, and in the Bulletin of 1878, Neroutsos wrote *Anno* without broken lines.

we find AVGVSTI interpolated where it never existed, and BARBARVS
is written in the Latin without the slightest hint that any difficulty
attended the reading. It is true that this is now proved to be
correct, but such treatment of an inscription reminds us too strongly
of Muratori to be palatable.

While waiting to obtain Mommsen's " Ephemeris Epigraphica," I
turn to the files of the London *Times* to see what attention the inscription received in England when the companion obelisk was
brought to London. From Commander Gorringe's " Obelisks " I had
learned only that Mr. Dixon had seen it. The story is best told by
the following extracts :

From the issue of July 4, 1877. A telegram from Paris says :
" An Alexandrian letter in the Cologne *Gazette* states that on laying
bare the socle of the obelisk about to be removed to London, Mr.
Dixon discovered a Greek and Latin inscription to the effect that
Barbarus, Governor of Egypt, erected the obelisk through the archi-
tect Pontius, in the eighth year of Augustus."

October 15, 1877. This issue contained a review of a pamphlet
on the obelisks, just published by Dr. Erasmus Wilson, through whose
munificence the London obelisk was conveyed to its present site.
" Mr. Wilson has done well to rectify the first interpretation put upon
the interesting monumental date of the erection of the pair of obelisks
before the Water-Gate of the Cæsareum at Alexandria, which was
found on the bronze supports of the standing obelisk during the opera-
tions for removal of the British Needle. They were set up in the
eighth year of Augustus, which was referred erroneously to the Italian
era of the emperor, B.C. 27, instead of to the local era of Alexandria,
B.C. 30, giving B.C. 23, as our author says. . . . Cleopatra might have
designed their removal from Heliopolis, as she may have designed
the temple of Cæsar itself."

November 19, 1877. A lecture was delivered by Mr. Dixon, on
the obelisk.

November 22, 1877. The British Archæological Association
held a meeting last night, at which Mr. Birch, Keeper of Oriental
Antiquities in the British Museum, lectured on " The Obelisk known
as Cleopatra's Needle." The Chairman (George Goodwin, F.R.S.,

F.S.A., V.P.), having introduced that gentleman as the greatest of our hieroglyphic scholars, and therefore the most competent to instruct us on the subject, Dr. Birch, in the course of his address, described more particularly the Alexandrian obelisks and their inscriptions. He also spoke of the date recorded on Cleopatra's Needle as that of the erection of the obelisk. . . . At the close of the lecture Mr. Dixon made some remarks on the shipping of the obelisk, and on his discovery of the Greek and Latin inscriptions on either side of the claw of one of the bronze crabs supporting the standing Needle. His observations were illustrated by photographs and enlarged diagrams.

April 10, 1878. Two days ago Professor Donaldson lectured on the obelisk before the Royal Institute of British Architects.

August 7, 1878. Dr. Birch furnishes a complete translation of the hieroglyphics of the obelisk.

September 13, 1878. The obelisk was erected upon the Thames Embankment yesterday. It was set up at Alexandria in the eighth year of Augustus, B.C. 23, along with the still-standing Needle, in front of the Sea-Gate of the temple founded by the beautiful queen in honor of her lover, the deified Julius, on occasion of the birth of her son Cæsarion.

September 14, 1878. The objects deposited in the core of the obelisk pedestal were copies of "Engineering," printed on vellum, with plans of the various arrangements and details employed in erecting and transporting the obelisk, together with its complete history.

In the meantime, the war over the site for the obelisk had been carried on by innumerable letters from Wilson, Palgrave, Lord Harrowby, R. A. Procter, and others, but no word of warning that the date of the inscriptions might be wrong appears to have been spoken.

October 21, 1878. Upon the base of the obelisk are to be affixed bronze plates bearing inscriptions, of which the text is prepared by such scholars as Dr. Birch and Dean Stanley, and approved by her Majesty. They have been referred to a committee of the Metropolitan Board of Works. Facing the roadway, the inscription is to read thus: "This obelisk . . . removed to Alexandria, the royal city of

Cleopatra. It was erected in the seventh (sic)' year of Augustus Cæsar, B.C 23."

January 31, 1882. The bronze inscribed tablets are ready to be affixed. The inscription is as follows: " Removed during the Greek dynasty to Alexandria, the royal city of Cleopatra. It was erected in the ninth (sic)' year of Augustus Cæsar, B.C. 23."

February 14, 1882. The tablets were affixed last week.

Here, side by side with the inscriptions in London, it may be proper to place those on our own obelisk touching the same point. On the restored crab at the southeast corner, we read on the right claw:

<table>
<tr><td>(Outside)</td><td>(Inside)</td></tr>
<tr><td>" L H KAIΣAPOΣ</td><td>ANNO VIII</td></tr>
<tr><td>BAPBAPOΣ ANEΘHKE</td><td>AVGVSTI CAESARIS</td></tr>
<tr><td>APXITEKTONOYNTOΣ</td><td>BARBARVS PRAEF</td></tr>
<tr><td>ΠONTIOY</td><td>AEGYPTI POSVIT</td></tr>
<tr><td></td><td>ARCHITECTANTE PONTIO</td></tr>
</table>

Reproduced from the original."

At the northeast corner, the right claw of the crab has, " Removed to Alexandria and erected there B.C. 22 by the Romans."

The dates now inscribed on the two obelisks will, therefore, be seen to differ by a year, and, under the former reading, ours was more likely to be right, in the proportion of two to one, as has already been shown; but this resulted from copying Neroutsos' original error of reckoning the beginning of the reign of Augustus from 29 instead of 30 B.C. It is to be hoped that, when the proper corrections are made, which will be rendered necessary now that the true date has been ascertained, both countries will either write the date 13–12, or they will agree upon one or the other of the two years, so that the two obelisks may be in harmony upon this point at least.

Having obtained, through the kindness of friends, a copy of the " Ephemeris Epigraphica," in which Mommsen had published our inscription in 1879, we will now examine his treatment of the subject. He first quotes a description of the crab from Neroutsos, which, after asserting that only one of the bronze supports still remained in position under the obelisk, closes with the extraordinary statement that " the claw of the crab, with the inscriptions, was carried off, as it ap-

---

¹ Typographical error.

pears, a few days after the discovery." [1] Then, after quoting the inscriptions exactly as given by Lumbroso, Mommsen says: " Neroutsos published this first in an Alexandrian paper, which Lepsius sent to me, then in the ' Bulletin de correspondance hellénique,' 1 (1877), p. 377, 2 (1878), p. 175 seq. I republished it from there in ' Staatsrecht,' 2', p. x. adn. The same prefect is named in the Greek inscription of Philæ of the year 13–12 B.C., published by Wescher (as above, p. 19). Since it is now established from these two inscriptions that Barbarus was prefect in Egypt before the 29th of August, B.C. 22, and remained in the same office at least till B.C. 13, it follows that my remarks upon the ' Monumentum Ancyranum,' p. 74, in relation to the first prefects of Egypt, are strengthened and confirmed. For I there stated that Cornelius Gallus was prefect to about 27; that Ælius Gallus followed him through the years 26–24; then Petronius governed the province during 23–22; all which agrees aptly with these inscriptions, provided we assume that the second expedition of Petronius against the Ethiopians in 22 was finished before the month of August of that year, which nothing hinders."

---

[1] " La pince du crabe avec les inscriptions a été enlevée, à ce qu'il paraît, quelques jours après la découverte." Since this was written I have succeeded in getting possession of the two articles of Neroutsos himself in the " Bulletin de correspondance hellénique," and find a solution for his strange supposition. The passage quoted above appears in a foot-note, of which Mommsen gives only a part. It continues as follows : " In a photograph of the exposed base of the obelisk, taken just before the earth that had been removed was replaced as before, one sees only the mutilated and disfigured body of the crab, without a vestige of the claw in question." This photograph must be the same as that given by Commander Gorringe (" Obelisks," plate iv.), and the crab there visible was the one situated at the corner diagonally opposite to that containing the inscription, and answers to the description of Neroutsos. It is probable that when he read the inscription the excavation beneath the obelisk was not completed, and this led him to suppose that only one of the crabs still remained. Entire removal of the accumulation revealed the other, and both are now preserved in the Metropolitan Museum of Art, and photographs of them can be seen in Gorringe's " Obelisks," plate v., where the inscriptions are also visible in much the same form as when this investigation was begun. There is a point of importance in both articles of Neroutsos which must not be omitted. In the first, written in modern Greek, he says, " While Mr. Dixon was removing the incrustation from the right claw of the crab I read at first dimly, then more clearly (ἀμυδρῶς τὸ πρῶτον καὶ ἔπειτα καθαρώτερον), the double inscription." In the second, written in French, he speaks more explicitly : " While Mr. Dixon was removing, by the aid of acids, the thick crust which covered the crab, I read, etc. (Pendant que M. Dixon enlevait à l'aide d'acides la rouille epaissé qui couvrait le crabe, je lisais . . .)."

Truly, this inscription experienced a curious series of unhappy adventures at the hands of the learned of the nineteenth century, within a few months after it was unearthed from its long seclusion. Not only did the inscription itself have to suffer in its integrity, but chronology, epigraphy, and history must needs be tortured and racked out of all resemblance to their former selves, to cover inaccuracy, support conjecture, or maintain pre-existing theories. Like the slaves of the ancients, they were not permitted to give their testimony save under stress of wheel and thumb-screw, and naturally the evidence obtained is no less worthless than much of that must necessarily have been which was extorted by such means from those hapless witnesses.

In his treatment of the testimony of Strabo, Mommsen's error, which vitiates his whole theory of these prefectures, is threefold, corresponding exactly to the three points in which the Geographer brings the events of his narrative into relation with occurrences elsewhere, when he says, namely, that the first Ethiopian expedition of Petronius was undertaken while Ælius was in Arabia; that his prisoners were despatched to Augustus, who had lately returned from Spain; and that the envoys of Candace, sent at the close of the second expedition, found Augustus in Samos, where he spent the winter of B.C. 21–20. The first of these points will be treated below; in the second, Mommsen inclines to throw more weight upon the indefinite "lately" (νεωστί) than it can bear, although his arrangement removes it about two years; the third he totally ignores. As for Dio, if he is not satisfied to adjust himself to the position in which Mommsen places him, he must shift for himself. By the results of the present investigation Strabo is completely vindicated, as he deserves to be for his exceeding care about matters of which he had personal knowledge.

Mommsen had hastened to publish our inscription from the Alexandrian paper in his "Staatsrecht," as quoted above, in 1877, for the purpose of refuting the supposition of Friedländer that the reign of Augustus in Egypt was reckoned from the year 43 B.C., a result which is secured equally by the inscription with its proper date. This supposition, however, needs no such refutation, and indeed was originally advanced to account for the strange coins that have been found with the date of the forty-sixth year of Augustus. These dates should be compared with the statement of Clemens Alexandrinus (p. 863), who, after fixing the length of the reign of Augustus at forty-three years, says that some make his reign forty-six years, four months, and one day. This would make the year of beginning B.C. 33, about the 18th of April, and it was about this time that Antony left Egypt to make his preparations against Augustus, and he did not return except as a vanquished and broken man after Actium. It seems possible that some of the flatterers of Augustus may have reckoned his reign from this circumstance. Eusebius sets the era of Augustus, reckoned from B.C. 43, in contrast with his Egyptian era, reckoned from 30, showing that the former was not Egyptian.[1]

Inasmuch as the question of the prefecture of Petronius has now assumed such proportions in this discussion, it may be well to treat the matter more in detail, even at the expense of some repetition. No ancient author declares distinctly who succeeded Cornelius in B.C. 26, and Dio styles Ælius Gallus prefect when speaking of the Arabian expedition;[2] but this very fact seems to show that he has made the mistake of calling him prefect before he actually became such, if, indeed, his language really implies that he was prefect at that time. It is idle to assume, as Mommsen does,[3] that he would have retained his position as prefect upon an expedition whose scope was so great as to include not only Arabia but Ethiopia, granting that he had been prefect before. But besides that, we have the testimony of Strabo, supported by Dio, that Petronius was prefect while Ælius was in Arabia, which effectually silences Mommsen's supposition. Zonaras and Xiphilinus also name Ælius prefect when speaking of his expedition; but here, as so often, Zonaras is simply copying Dio, as is plain from the cast of his language, while Xiphilinus pretends to do nothing but epitomize Dio. Dio flourished more than two hundred years after the Arabian expedition, and Zonaras eleven hundred. But take the writers near the epoch of the events themselves, and not one of them calls Ælius prefect during the expedition. Strabo styles

---

[1] Hist. Eccles. i. 5.
[2] liii. 29 : ἐπὶ Ἀραβίαν . . . Αἴλιος Γάλλος ὁ τῆς Αἰγύπτου ἄρχων ἐπεστράτευσε.
[3] Res Gest. Div. Aug., p. 76.

him prefect twice (118, 806) when he is describing their tour together
through the province to Syene; but when speaking of his expedition into Arabia (118, 780, 781, 819, 820) he never gives him this
title. Once he designates him simply Ælius Gallus, while on the
tour (816) having already called him prefect. Pliny is equally ex-
plicit. Of Ælius, in Arabia, he mentions only his equestrian rank;[1]
but of Petronius, in Ethiopia, he is careful to add that he was prefect
of Egypt.[2] Similarly, Josephus and Galen speak of Ælius in connection with his expedition, but do not call him prefect; while Josephus does denominate Petronius prefect when speaking of the corn
sent to Herod. This seems to show that Dio's is simply a careless
expression, as was remarked above.

The known facts belonging to the prefecture of Petronius are
these: the great work of clearing out all the canals of Egypt, more
or less blocked by the gradual accumulation of sediment, so that
when this was accomplished a rise of three feet less than before in
the Nile would still produce the most abundant crops, while no famine ensued as before if the minimum limit of eight cubits was
reached;[3] repressing a riot in Alexandria;[4] sending abundance of
corn to Herod in the time of the famine; finally, the two Ethiopian
expeditions, and despatching at the end of the first one thousand
prisoners to Augustus, and at the end of the second, the envoys
of Candace likewise to the emperor, then in Samos.[5] Now, the se-
quence of events which seems to me to harmonize best with the several accounts of his prefecture is this: in the first place, that he succeeded Cornelius in 26, and that the clearing of the canals occupied
the first two years of his office. This accords not only with the order of events followed by Strabo, but with the statement of Sueto-
nius,[6] that this great "triumph of man over nature," as Strabo terms
it, was achieved by the labors of the soldiers (*militari opere*). Two
years seem scarcely too short for the work, and no time was so suit-
able for it as this period, when he had the full force of three legions
to employ upon it. During the remainder of his prefecture this

[1] vi. 32: Ælius Gallus ex equestri ordine.
[2] vi. 35: duce P. Petronio, et ipso equestris ordinis præfecto Ægypti.
[3] Strabo, 788.   [4] Ibid. 819.   [5] Ibid. 820, 821.   [6] Aug. 18.

force was diminished by the Arabian expedition and employed in the Ethiopian campaigns. The time of the riot is impossible to fix, but, according to the order of events, as narrated by Strabo, it would fall into the period before the expedition of Ælius. Following Dio[1] and Josephus, we shall fix the departure of Ælius and his force from Alexandria in the summer of 24. We know from Pliny (vi. 26) that it was customary for voyagers to start for Arabia and India about the 1st of August. Reaching Cleopatris (Suez), at the head of the Red Sea, about this time, Ælius discovered that a great blunder had been committed. The eighty ships that had been constructed for the expedition were found to be totally unsuited for the kind of voyage to be undertaken, and one hundred and thirty lighter craft had to be built in their stead. This was the first great mistake of the campaign, as Strabo says,[2] and I am convinced from his language that it was not discovered until the arrival at Cleopatris, and that the force had to remain there through the winter while the other ships were building.[3] It may well have been during this stay that Herod sent his five hundred auxiliaries to join the expedition, in return for the assistance he received from Petronius during the famine. The fact that the grain sowed in the first year of famine (B.C. 25) would not come up in the following season (as Josephus tells us it did not) would be ascertained some time before the close of Herod's thirteenth year (4th of April, 24), since in that climate the barley is *ready to be cut* about the 1st of April; and as Herod was a man both bold in emergency and prompt to act, his preparations to send to Egypt for corn would certainly have been made in the early spring, not "after the summer was over" (*post aestatem*), as Mommsen says, thinking of Germany rather than Palestine. Moreover, in the following year (23, Herod's fifteenth) his affairs were in so prosperous a

[1] In fixing the time consumed upon this expedition, every one is compelled to desert the lead of Dio, who seems to limit its continuance to a single year (liii. 29). His statement cannot stand for an instant by the side of Strabo's circumstantial account. As is usual with historians, he assigns the beginning of the expedition to its proper year, and finishes the account of the whole before turning to another subject, without properly distinguishing its duration, as he does also in the case of the events in Ethiopia.

[2] 780: πρῶτον μὲν δὴ τοῦθ' ἁμάρτημα συνέβη.

[3] Compare Merivale, Hist. Rome, iv. 121.

condition that he spent vast sums in repairing the temple at Jerusalem and in building a palace for himself, one apartment of which he named after Augustus, another after Agrippa.[1]

Accordingly, it is after the winter of 24–23 that Ælius at last sets sail from Cleopatris with ten thousand Roman troops and his auxiliaries, and, after a tempestuous voyage of fifteen days, arrives at Leuce-Come, in Arabia, where he was compelled to pass the summer and winter,[2] in consequence of the maladies which had attacked his troops. In the spring of 22 he started out for the interior and was led by circuitous routes, so that he spent six months upon the advance,[3] but accomplished his return to the coast in sixty days.[4] Thence he passed over to Myos Hormos in eleven days, and then travelled across country to the Nile at Coptos. This distance is stated by Pliny (vi. 26) as two hundred and fifty-seven miles, over a mountainous district, which was traversed in twelve days by the merchants, and probably not much less by the force of Ælius, in their wretched condition. From Coptos to Alexandria it is three hundred and eight miles, according to Pliny, and required about twelve days. Hence, nine full months must have been occupied by Ælius in reaching Alexandria after starting out from Leuce-Come in the spring, so that it must have been very near the end of the year 22 when he returned. Consequently, Mommsen's statement, that he consumed a year or a little more on the expedition, is lengthened out by Strabo into a summer, a winter, and nine months besides, from the time they sailed from Cleopatris.

Following Dio again, we shall place the descent of the Ethiopians upon Syene in the early part of 22, which brings us again into harmony with Strabo and the crucial fact, which Mommsen ignores in the main, and renders improbable by his disposition of events, that it was *while* and *because* the Roman force was weakened by the withdrawal of the troops with Ælius, that the Ethiopians made their incursion.

[1] Joseph. Bel. Jud. i. 21.
[2] Strabo, 781 : τὸ θέρος καὶ τὸν χείμωνα.
[3] Strabo, 782 ἐξ δὶ μηνῶν χρόνον ἐν ταῖς ὁδοῖς κατέτριψε.
[4] **Ibid.** : τὴν πᾶσαν ὁδὸν ἑξηκοσταῖος ἐξήνυσε κατὰ τὴν ἐπάνοδον.

The route probably pursued by Petronius through Ethiopia is well described by Kenrick ("Ancient Egyptians") as that now most commonly followed by caravans and travellers. Keeping the river to Pselchis (Dekki) about sixty miles, and thence to Korusko, fifty miles more, a mountain pass opens into the valley of the Nile, leading through the desert by a route of about two hundred and fifty miles to Abou Hammed (Premnis), where it rejoins the river just at the beginning of the great bend to the southwest. The first sixty miles of this route is through a valley with some vegetation; then follows the desert in all its horrors for fifty miles, through which Petronius passed on his way to Premnis, "making his way," as Strabo says, "through the sands where the army of Cambyses was overwhelmed."[1] The remaining distance is over a region of barren rock.

Before withdrawing from Ethiopia Petronius fortified Premnis, victualled it for two years, and left a garrison of four hundred men. Such an expedition would necessarily consume the greater part of the year 22. Upon his return to Alexandria he sold some of his prisoners, sent one thousand to Augustus, and diseases carried off the rest. These events may reasonably be supposed to carry us into the next year, as indeed Mommsen acknowledges, and I am happy to find one point upon which I can agree with him in this matter. Hereupon, news arrives in Alexandria that Candace has attacked Premnis with many myriads. Petronius leads his forces a second time thither, and when he has strengthened the place still further, the Ethiopians open negotiations with him; but he tells them they must treat with Cæsar in person. Upon their declaring that they did not know who Cæsar was, nor where they must go to find him, he gave them guides to conduct them, and they went to Samos, where Cæsar was *on the point of setting out for Syria* in the spring of 20.[2] They were kindly received by the emperor, "obtained all that they asked, and even the tribute which had been laid upon them was remitted."[3] It is probable

---

[1] Strabo, 820: ἐυλθὼν τοὺς θῖνας, ἐν οἷς ὁ Καμβύσου κατεχώσθη στρατός.

[2] This incident in the narrative seems to show that the envoys did not reach Alexandria in 21, at least till the close of navigation, which fell about the first of October (Acts xxvii. 9; Joseph. Antiq. Jud. iii. 10; Philo ad Caium, 3. in Flacc. 15), and for some four months in winter all vessels were kept in harbor (Hor. C. i. 4, iii. 7).

[3] Strabo, 820, 821: τὴν δὲ Πρῆμνιν τειχίσας βέλτιον, φρουρὰν ἰμβαλὼν καὶ τροφὴν ἐνεῖν ἐνιαυτῶν

that among their requests was the withdrawal of the Romans from
Premnis, which would naturally follow from their being released from
the tribute, Augustus being "sensible of the fruitlessness of attempt-
ing to extend his sway into their wild regions," as Merivale judiciously
remarks.[1]

Petronius had now held the prefecture for a long term, and his
recent exploits in Ethiopia had made him too conspicuous a person
to be left there longer. Augustus had had sufficient experience
already in the case of Cornelius Gallus to render him especially
sensitive in regard to Egypt; and as he was making his eastern tour
for the special purpose of arranging matters for some time to come,
we may suppose that Petronius was now honorably recalled and sent
to Rome. If we follow Pliny, who calls him P. Petronius instead of
C., as Dio names him, we shall not go wrong in identifying him with
P. Petronius Turpilianus, who was one of the masters of the mint in
20–19, and struck numerous coins bearing his name. One of these
on the reverse bears the legend AVGVSTVS CAESAR, and represents
a person standing in a chariot drawn by two elephants, and holding
a laurel branch and a sceptre. Some similar coins were issued with
the names also of his colleagues Durmius and Aquillius.[2] In these
coins the elephants have usually been taken as an allusion to India;
but they may, with much greater reason, be referred to the recent
victories in Ethiopia. It should be observed that they have no
legend relating to Armenia and Parthia, as many others issued by
the same mint-masters, and they agree in presenting the very unusual order in the name as above, Augustus before Cæsar instead of
after it.

The appointment of Ælius to succeed Petronius may well be
explained by a desire of Augustus to throw a veil over his ill-success

τιτρακοσίοις ἀνέρασιν, ἀπῇρεν εἰς ᾿Αλεξάνρριαν· καὶ τῶν αἰχμαλώτων τοὺς μὲν ἰλαφρροπώλησι, χιλίους
δὲ Καίσαρι ἔπεμψε νεωστὶ ἐκ Κανράβρων ἥκοντι, τοὺς δὲ νόσοι διεχρήσαντο. ἐν τούτῳ μυσιάσι Κανδάκη
πολλαῖς ἐπὶ τὴν φρουρὰν ἐπῆλθε· Πετρώνιος δ᾿ ἐξεβοήθησι καὶ φθάνει προσελθὼν εἰς τὸ φρούριον, καὶ
πλείοσι παρασκειναῖς ἐξασφαλισάμενος τὸν τόπον, πρεσβιυσαμένων, ἐκέλευσιν ὡς Καίσαρα πρεσβεύεσθαι·
οὐκ εἰδέναι δὲ φασκόντων ὅστις εἴη Καίσαρ καὶ ὅπη βαδιστέον εἴη παρ᾿ αὐτόν, ἔδωκε τοὺς παραπέμψοντας·
καὶ ἧκον εἰς Σάμον, ἐνταῦθα τοῦ Καίσαρος ὄντος καὶ μέλλοντος εἰς Συρίαν ἐντεῦθιν προϊέναι, Τιβέριον
εἰς Ἀρμενίαν στέλλοντος. πάντων δὲ τυχόντων ὧν ἐδέοντο, ἀφῆκεν αὐτοὺς καὶ τοὺς φόρους οἷς ἐπέστησι.

    [1] Hist. Rome, iv. p. 127.   [2] Cohen, Descrip. des Monnaies.

in Arabia by his promotion; and in the "Monumentum Ancyranum," the great memorial written by the emperor just before his death, detailing his exploits, he places side by side as distinguished achievements the expeditions into Arabia and Ethiopia, which took place "at about the same time" (*eodem fere tempore*), as he says, thus agreeing with Strabo with sufficient exactness.

In relation to the architect Pontius, Professor Lumbroso, in his account of the inscriptions, gives us some interesting information. He says: "The mention of the architect Pontius is worthy of observation, since the coincidence of time leads us to compare the name with that of the artist who designed the beautiful fountain recently discovered on the site of the Gardens of Mæcenas,' which shows so strongly the influence of Alexandrian art."

The find here meant is a marble drinking-horn, or cornucopia,² about four feet in length, with the upper part excavated to contain fruits or flowers, it is supposed, its smaller end terminating in a bizarre chimæra. The horn is supported upon a plinth out of which acanthus leaves are springing, as if to form a bed for its repose. An orifice is cut to receive a pipe from below and conduct the water so as to issue in a jet from beneath the bended knees of the chimæra. Its use as an ornament for a fountain is plain. Upon a small band in front is engraved the inscription,

ΠΟΝΤΙΟΣ ΑΘΗΝΑΙΟΣ ΕΠΟΙΕΙ.

Around the upper portion of the horn, beneath the rim, is a row of three Mænads in various attitudes of Bacchic frenzy, together with a Bacchic crater, or mixing-bowl. The execution of the figures is exquisite, in gesture, pose, and drapery; but they are proved by comparison with other remains of antiquity to be copies of celebrated pieces and not original designs. This fact, together with the form of the Λ in the inscription (which is exactly like that in ΒΑΡΒΑΡΟΣ, both at Alexandria and Philæ), the use of the imperfect ΕΠΟΙΕΙ, instead of

¹ Bull. d. Comm. Arch. Munic. 1875, p. 118.
² The cornucopia was selected by Ptolemy Philadelphus, according to Athenæus (497), as the special symbol of Arsinoe, and it appears frequently upon Ptolemaic coins, as occasionally on those of Augustus. It was a favorite symbol with Horace (C. i. 17, 16; C. S. 60; Epl. i. 12, 29.)

the aorist ΕΠΟΙΗΣΕ, and the site upon which it was found, has led
the archæologists of Rome to the conclusion that the monument
belongs certainly to the time of Mæcenas.

Hence, from the evidence now before us, we may outline the career of Pontius with some confidence in this way. Of Athenian birth,
he passed over to Alexandria to study and pursue his chosen profession
in that more enterprising capital. Proving himself a man of note as
an architect, Barbarus, with his help, conceived the idea of transporting
two of the obelisks of Heliopolis to Alexandria, and erecting them
there before the temple. The fame of his success in achieving this
difficult task in 13–12 (the first of the kind under the Romans), was
carried to Rome, and the emperor was induced to attempt the still
more difficult feat of transporting two more obelisks to the Capitol.
The feeling with which this achievement was regarded is expressed
by Pliny (xxxvi. 14). After mentioning the two obelisks as standing
before the temple in Alexandria, he proceeds to say that "the difficulty of conveying these monoliths to Rome by sea surpassed everything, and the vessels used were marvellous spectacles, so that Augustus consecrated the first one at Puteoli." We can now see rightly, for
the first time, the connection in the mind of Pliny between the obelisks
at Alexandria and those of Augustus at Rome; for the inscriptions
that have been discovered on the bases of the last prove that they
were erected in B.C. 10–9, three years after those at Alexandria.[1] That
Pontius was engaged upon this task we have no express information;
but it is natural to suppose that the architect who had been so suc-
cessful in the first attempt would be the person selected for the second so soon after; and when we find the name again upon the fountain in the Gardens of Mæcenas, we may continue the sketch of his
career by supposing that he was the person chosen for the task, and,

---

[1] Orelli, 36 ; C. I. L. vi, 701 :

IMP.CAESAR.DIVI.F.
AVGVSTVS
PONTIFEX MAXIMVS
IMP.XII.COS.XI.TRIB.POT.XIV.
AEGVPTO.IN.POTESTATEM
POPVLI.ROMANI.REDACTA
SOLI.DONVM.DEDIT.

after he had finished these gigantic labors, he turned his hand to the beautiful trifle now discovered in the gardens of the great prime-minister of Augustus, out of gratitude to whose munificent patronage of artists and poets he might well have been glad to execute such a commission. But he rewarded himself by inscribing his name even here, as upon the base of the obelisk at Alexandria. We may fondly think that Mæcenas, who died B.C. 8, was the good friend of Pontius, as well as of Horace, and that the poet and the statesman may many a time, in the last year of their lives, have gazed admiringly upon the handiwork of their friend, the architect Pontius.

Respectfully yours,

Augustus C. Merriam.

LIDDELL & SCOTT'S GREEK-ENGLISH LEXICON.

A GREEK-ENGLISH LEXICON. Compiled by HENRY GEORGE LIDDELL, D.D., Dean of Christ Church, Oxford, and ROBERT SCOTT, D.D., Dean of Rochester, late Master of Balliol College, Oxford. Seventh Edition, Revised and Augmented throughout, with the Co-operation of Professor DRISLER, of Columbia College, New York. 4to, Sheep, $10 00.

It is truly a magnificent work, both in its exterior form and in its contents. It would be difficult to say wherein it falls short of the *ideal* of a Greek-English lexicon.—Professor W. S. TYLER, *Amherst College.*

A work which has stood the test of forty years' constant use at the hands of the best scholars here and in England needs little characterization of its many and acknowledged excellences. It is sufficient to say that it is without doubt the best Greek-English lexicon in our language, and that it is fully abreast of the best scholarship of the two countries. —*Christian Union*, N. Y.

It would be difficult to name any dictionary which has done more for any branch of literature or science than that which is the subject of this article. Partly by their own labors, and partly by availing themselves of those of others, Dean Liddell and Dean Scott have brought their lexicon to a degree of excellence which has the appearance of finality, if finality is possible of attainment in lexicography.—*London Times.*

A Greek-English lexicon as nearly perfect as can well be hoped for in many a year to come. No Greek scholar in either England or America can afford to be without it.—President R. D. HITCHCOCK, in the *Evangelist,* N. Y.

It is now the best product of its kind ; the representative work of an age which represents the highest point of Greek scholarship ever reached in England. Nearly every page shows signs of addition, improvement, and skilful compression, and that to an extent that would hardly have been supposed practicable, did not the fact abundantly appear on comparison with the former editions.— *Sunday-School Times,* Philadelphia.

A noble monument of critical scholarship and patient industry ; and will still further facilitate the acquisition of the noble tongue whose usages it illustrates.—*Literary World,* Boston.

This work, as it stands, is a monument of modern classical scholarship, and it is hard to conceive of a dictionary more complete, exact, and full in its references.—*Christian at Work,* N. Y.

It is a monument of patient scholarship, and is a blessing to every classical student.—*Journal of Education,* Boston.

So nearly perfect that one can hardly see what chances there are for improvement in any future edition.—*Boston Transcript.*

It seems to furnish in its present form all that is necessary in a critical and accurate lexicon of the Greek language.—Dr. HENRY A. COIT, *St. Paul's School,* Concord, N. H.

It is impossible to doubt that this lexicon is not only an improvement on the last issue so great as to make an epoch, but also the best that we shall have for many years to come.— *The Critic,* N. Y.

This great dictionary embodies the best Greek scholarship of the era, and becomes the final appeal in the interpretation of the New Testament, as well as the classic Greek. Students of the sacred Scriptures will appreciate the broad and accurate scholarship, and the long, persistent studies of the authors of this great work ; and every advanced student will look upon the possession of this invaluable Greek thesaurus as indispensable to his critical apparatus.—*Zion's Herald,* Boston.

A Greek-English lexicon in respect to its matter and standing unrivalled and alone in England and the United States.—*N. Y. Times.*

The work now embodies all the results of modern Greek scholarship with whatever has come from the study of comparative philology. It is a monument of patient labor and broad and accurate learning, and its typographical arrangement is such as to be specially helpful to the student.—*Boston Journal.*

The recognition of American scholarship in its preparation will be appreciated in this country. The republic of letters knows of no political divisions.—*Watchman,* Boston.

That portion of the book connected with comparative philology has been entirely recast, in harmony with the strides that have been made in that science since the first editions of the lexicon appeared. — *Saturday Evening Gazette,* Boston.

PUBLISHED BY HARPER & BROTHERS, NEW YORK.

☞ HARPER & BROTHERS *will send the above work by mail, postage prepaid, to any part of the United States, on receipt of the price.*

SOME USEFUL BOOKS OF REFERENCE.

Haydn's Dictionary of Dates.
Haydn's Dictionary of Dates and Universal Information relating to all Ages and Nations. Seventeenth Edition, containing the History of the World to the Autumn of 1881. By BENJAMIN VINCENT. Revised for American Readers. Large 8vo, 810 pages, Cloth, $5 00.

Skeat's Etymological Dictionary.
A Concise Etymological Dictionary of the English Language. By the Rev. WALTER W. SKEAT, M.A. 12mo, Cloth, Uniform with "The Student's Series," $1 25.

Crabb's English Synonymes.
English Synonymes Explained in Alphabetical Order. With copious Illustrations and Examples drawn from the Best Writers. To which is now added an Index to the Words. By GEORGE CRABB, A.M. New Edition, with Additions and Corrections. 12mo, 856 pages, Cloth, $2 50.

Reber's Ancient Art.
History of Ancient Art. By Dr. FRANZ VON REBER. Revised by the Author. Translated and Augmented by JOSEPH THACHER CLARKE. With 310 Illustrations and a Glossary of Technical Terms. 8vo, Cloth, $3 50.

Schliemann's Ilios.
Ilios, the City and Country of the Trojans. The Results of Researches and Discoveries on the Site of Troy and throughout the Troad in the years 1871–'72–'73, '78, '79; including an Autobiography of the Author. By Dr. HENRY SCHLIEMANN, F.S.A. With a Preface, Appendices, and Notes. With Maps, Plans, and about 1800 Illustrations. Imperial 8vo, Cloth, $12 00.

Cesnola's Cyprus.
Cyprus: its Ancient Cities, Tombs, and Temples. A Narrative of Researches and Excavations during Ten Years' Residence in that Island. By General LOUIS PALMA DI CESNOLA. With Portrait, Maps, and 400 Illustrations. 8vo, Cloth, Extra, Gilt Tops and Uncut Edges, $7 50.

Mahaffy's Greek Literature.
A History of Classical Greek Literature. By J. P. MAHAFFY. In Two Volumes. 12mo, Cloth, $4 00.

Simcox's Latin Literature.
A History of Latin Literature, from Ennius to Boethius. By GEORGE AUGUSTUS SIMCOX, M.A. In Two Volumes. 12mo, Cloth, $4 00.

Symonds's Studies of the Greek Poets.
Studies of the Greek Poets. By JOHN ADDINGTON SYMONDS. Revised and Enlarged by the Author. In Two Volumes. Square 16mo, Cloth, $3 50.

Muller's Political History of Recent Times.
Political History of Recent Times (1816–1875). With Special Reference to Germany. By WILHELM MÜLLER, Professor in Tübingen. Revised and Enlarged by the Author. Translated, with an Appendix covering the Period from 1876 to 1881, by the Rev. JOHN P. PETERS, Ph.D. 12mo, Cloth, $3 00.

PUBLISHED BY HARPER & BROTHERS, NEW YORK.

☞ Any of the above books sent by mail, postage prepaid, to any part of the United States, on receipt of the price.

www.ingramcontent.com/pod-product-compliance
Lightning Source LLC
Chambersburg PA
CBHW031804090426

42739CB00008B/1161